# EBOX

## Marc Zabludoff

**Marshall Cavendish**
Benchmark

New York

Published by Marshall Cavendish Benchmark
An imprint of Marshall Cavendish Corporation

Other Marshall Cavendish Offices:
Marshall Cavendish International (Asia) Private Limited, 1 New Industrial Road, Singapore 536196 • Marshall Cavendish International (Thailand) Co Ltd. 253 Asoke, 12th Flr, Sukhumvit 21 Road, Klongtoey Nua, Wattana, Bangkok 10110, Thailand • Marshall Cavendish (Malaysia) Sdn Bhd, Times Subang, Lot 46, Subang Hi-Tech Industrial Park, Batu Tiga, 40000 Shah Alam, Selangor Darul Ehsan, Malaysia

Marshall Cavendish is a trademark of Times Publishing Limited

All websites were available and accurate when this book was sent to press.

Library of Congress Cataloguing-in-Publication Data

Zabludoff, Marc.
Ebox / by Marc Zabludoff.
p. cm. — (Green cars)
Includes bibliographical references and index.
Summary: "Provides information on the electric technology used in the eBox, and discusses how the green movement is affecting the auto industry"—Provided by publisher.
ISBN 978-1-60870-009-7
1. Scion xB automobile—Customizing—Juvenile literature. 2. Electric automobiles—Juvenile literature. 3. AC Propulsion (Firm)—Juvenile literature. I. Title.
TL215.S25Z33 2011
629.22'93—dc22
2009041717

Editor: Megan Comerford
Publisher: Michelle Bisson
Art Director: Anahid Hamparian
Series Designer: Daniel Roode

Illustration on pp. 26–27 by Alanna Ranellone

Photo research by Connie Gardner

Cover photo by Ron Kimball/www.kimballstock.com

The photographs in this book are used by permission and through the courtesy of: AC Propulsion: Henry Chea, 8, 40; Corbis: Car Culture, 11; AP Photo: Jeff Chin, 14; Mario Jose Sanchez, 17; Mark Lennihan, 36; Getty Images: Scott Olson, 20; Torsten Silz, 29; Vince Bucri, 32; Tom Hanks, 22; Ron Kimball/www.kimballstock.com: 30; Alamy: David Zanzinger, 38; Mark Scheuem, 41.

Printed in Malaysia (T)
135642

# Contents

# Introduction

Most cars in the world run on gasoline, and some cars use more gas than others. Gasoline is made from petroleum, or crude oil, which is a liquid buried deep in the earth. Petroleum formed naturally from the **decomposed** and **compressed** remains of tiny **organisms** that lived millions of years ago. Humans drill deep into the earth to take the oil out.

However, the amount of oil in the world is limited. The more we take out of the ground now, the less there will be in the future, and eventually it will run out. Taking it out of the ground is expensive and damages the **environment**.

Also, when oil and the products made from oil (gasoline, engine oil, heating oil, and diesel fuel) are burned, they give off pollution in the form of gases that damage the **atmosphere**. The carbon dioxide ($CO_2$) that gasoline-burning engines give off is one of the major causes of **global warming**.

Carbon dioxide is a **greenhouse gas**. Like the glass panes of a greenhouse, the gas traps heat. The build-up of carbon dioxide in the atmosphere, scientists warn, is keeping Earth's heat from escaping into space. As a result, the planet is warming up.

In the United States, about 90 percent of the greenhouse gases we produce is from burning oil, gasoline, and coal. One-third of this comes from the engines that power the vehicles we use to move people and objects around. If we do not stop this global warming, life on Earth could begin to get very uncomfortable.

The problem is not just that temperatures might rise a bit. A warming atmosphere could melt the ice of the Arctic and Antarctic, raise the level of water in the seas, and change the **climate** of many places on Earth. Animals unable to adjust to the new conditions might become extinct (die out). Plants and crops might no longer be able to grow where people need them. Many islands, low-lying countries, and communities along the coasts of all the continents might disappear into the sea.

Doesn't sound so good, does it? These problems are why many people are interested in **alternative fuels** that can power our cars and other engines with less or no pollution.

Now that you know that oil is made from living things that died a long time ago, it should be no surprise that people are making oil from live plants to power their cars. This fuel, called *biodiesel*, can

be made from soybean oil, canola oil, sunflowers, and other plants. One form of biodiesel is similar to the vegetable oil used for cooking. Some people gather or buy this used oil from restaurants and use it to power their cars. The engines in these cars have to be modified, or changed, in order to burn this oil correctly.

Another popular way to power cars is with batteries. Modern batteries are being made to be so powerful that some cars use them in combination with gas engines; this system is called *hybrid technology*. Hybrid cars have a gas engine and an electric motor. The electric motor usually takes over when the car runs at low speeds or when it stops.

Many auto engineers are designing electric cars that run only on batteries. Until recently, too many batteries were needed to make this an **efficient** technology. But there have been important advances in battery technology. The company Smart, for example, has developed an all-electric car that is in use in England.

Another form of alternative energy for cars is the hydrogen **fuel cell**, which gives off power when the hydrogen and oxygen in the fuel cell are combined. If we are to start driving hydrogen-powered cars, however, hydrogen fueling stations would have to be as common along U.S. roads and highways as gas stations are today.

Oil is a limited resource, costs a lot to extract, pollutes the land, air, and water, and forces most countries to rely on the few nations that have a plentiful supply of it. If the world wants to become a cleaner, safer place, developing alternative fuels to power at least some of our vehicles is extremely important.

The eBox is an all-electric vehicle that is made by AC Propulsion, a company dedicated to developing technology for electric cars. They hope the technology used to power the eBox will pave the way for mass-produced cars that are greener and more efficient than those available today.

The company's electric-vehicle technology is unique because it can be customized to any type of vehicle—not just the eBox. But the company is hoping to show people that electric cars are the future of transportation one eBox at a time.

# Chapter 1
# An Electrifying Idea

In theory, the eBox is a car that could both slow global warming and lessen America's dependency on foreign countries for oil. The eBox runs on electricity only. It burns no gasoline whatsoever, and therefore produces no gases that are harmful to the environment.

The eBox is not a car that is being produced in large numbers—there is no factory turning them out one after another on a long assembly line. Instead, the company AC Propulsion **converts** a gasoline-powered Toyota Scion xB into a fully electric vehicle with rechargeable batteries. The result is the eBox!

◀ **Engineers at AC Propulsion chose to convert a Scion xB into an electric car because of the vehicle's unique, eye-catching shape.**

## EXPERIMENTING WITH ELECTRICITY

AC Propulsion is headquartered in San Dimas, California, a city near car-clogged Los Angeles. The company was founded in 1992 by Alan Cocconi, an engineer who got his start with major American automaker General Motors (GM).

At GM Cocconi worked on developing an experimental electric car called the Impact. The Impact itself was never produced, but it became the basis for the EV1 (EV stands for "electric vehicle"), which GM introduced in California in 1997.

The EV1 was a marvel for its time. It could speed up to 123 miles per hour (198 kilometers per hour) and its batteries had enough juice to power the car for 90 miles (145 km). Many people loved the EV1, and they were disappointed when GM decided the car would always be too expensive to make and ended its short existence.

Long before that happened, though, Cocconi had moved on. He had decided that the time was right for a serious new look at battery-powered cars, but that big car companies, like GM, were too committed to making cars the same old way—with an internal combustion engine. An internal combustion engine burns gasoline inside to produce power. When the fuel is burned, smoke and gases, including carbon dioxide, are given off. These unused fumes are what come out of the tailpipe.

The 1991 Impact concept car was a sporty, futuristic-looking car. Engineers fine tuned the car's body and electric technology before releasing the EV1 in 1997.

# Record Breakers and Roadsters

Technological developments made by engineers at AC Propulsion have enabled other companies to also build electric cars, such as the White Lightning and the Tesla Roadster.

The White Lightning was built by Dempsey World Record Associates (DWRA) and is most famous for being the world's fastest electric car. In October 1999 it set the land speed record for electric vehicles, clocking a speed of 245.5 miles per hour (395 km/h). In 2000 DWRA completed the White Lightning II, which can travel at more than 300 miles per hour (483 km/h). It is powered by a 420-volt battery pack and two electric motors, designed by Alan Cocconi, that provide the equivalent of approximately 400 horsepower.

The Tesla Roadster is the fastest battery-powered production car, with a top speed of 125 miles per hour (201 km/h). When Tesla Motors was first founded, the company licensed a patent from AC Propulsion in order to start building their own power train.

The 2010 Roadster is powered by a 375-volt electric motor and a lithium-ion battery that charges in three and a half hours and has a charge range of 244 miles (393 km).

So Cocconi started his own company, one that would develop the technology to make electric cars possible. For the most part, that technology included a powerful electric motor and a reliable, rechargeable battery that could hold a lot of energy, be small enough to fit in a car frame, and be light enough to not weigh the car down.

# Chapter 2
# Under the Hood

**B**y 1994 Cocconi had developed an electric motor powerful enough and efficient enough for the car he imagined. Like all electric motors—and unlike all internal combustion engines—it could get up to maximum power almost instantly, so it promised a lot of "zoom."

Cocconi also developed the machinery he needed to regulate the flow of electricity from the batteries to the motor. He called his new **drive system** the T-150. His next goal was to put the T-150 into a car that could prove to the public that a battery-powered car could perform just as well as a gasoline-powered car.

◄ **An eBox was on display at the Plug-In 2008 conference in San Jose, California.**

## THE TZERO

The car he built was called the tzero (pronounced "tee-zero"). In experiments scientists call the starting point of an experiment $T_0$, which is an abbreviation for "time zero." This was a good name for Cocconi's car because it, too, was a starting point.

The tzero was an electric sports car, and it generated a lot of news when AC Propulsion unveiled it in 1996. The car could accelerate from 0 to 60 miles per hour (0 to 97 km/h) in a mere 4 seconds. It could travel at least 90 miles (145 km) before the batteries needed recharging.

Over the next several years, AC Propulsion perfected the tzero, and introduced a second version of the car in 2003. This time, the tzero could accelerate from 0 to 60 miles per hour (0 to 97 km/h) in only 3.6 seconds. The new version could travel 300 miles (483 km) without recharging, a big improvement over 90 miles.

What made the difference was a new kind of battery. The original tzero used lead-acid batteries, the same kind found in any gasoline-powered car. In a conventional car, a single lead-acid battery supplies power to such things as the lights and the radio— nothing terribly demanding.

AC Propulsion's tzero attracted a lot of attention in downtown Sonoma, California, in 2003.

In an electric car, though, the battery supplies power to the wheels also, and that drains the battery of its energy quickly. To achieve a good **range**, the first tzero needed twenty-eight lead-acid batteries, each one about the size of an encyclopedia, and weighing a little more than 36 pounds (16 kilograms). All together, they not only took up a lot of room but also added a lot of weight—more than 1,000 pounds (454 kg)—to the car.

The 2003 tzero used a smaller, lighter power source: lithium-ion batteries, similar to the kind used in laptop computers and cell phones. By packing together 6,800 individual batteries (each one slightly larger than a standard AA battery), the tzero's builders were able to shave 500 pounds (227 kg) off the weight of the car.

The lighter weight let it compete, in sprints, against powerful gas-guzzlers like Ferraris and Porsches. More important, the lithium-ion batteries made possible the birth of the far less flashy but far more practical offshoot of the tzero: the eBox.

## SCION XB TO EBOX

On the outside, the eBox hardly looks like the son of a racer. The Toyota Scion xB is a rectangular, blunt-sided car that looks more like a box on wheels than a sports car. In fact, the boxy frame of the Scion xB is the reason the electric conversion was dubbed the eBox—*e* for "electric" and *Box* because of the shape.

The well-built Scion xB was perfect for AC Propulsion's needs. Its boxy look appealed to younger drivers, who would most likely be the first to embrace a new kind of car. Also, the Scion xB not only had room for five people, but it also had room for the large lithium-ion battery pack. Finally, it was a Toyota, a brand that car buyers trusted.

When a Scion xB rolls out of the factory, it is a standard gasoline-powered car. It includes an internal combustion engine; a gas tank; a system of exhaust pipes for carrying gases from the engine away from the car; devices such as a catalytic converter, which turns some of the more dangerous gases into less harmful ones; and parts like the muffler, which reduces the noise made by the engine exhaust. When a Scion is turned into an eBox, the first thing that happens is that all those parts are removed.

## Fun Facts

AC Propulsion built only three tzero prototypes before deciding the $220,000 electric sports car would be too expensive to mass produce. Not many people can afford to go green at that price! All three prototypes are still running well.

Toyota designers made the Scion xB's body rounder for the 2008 model. But they made sure to keep the vehicle's recognizable shape!

An electric motor replaces the gas engine. A battery pack, made of 48 connected "modules" of lithium-ion batteries, replaces the gas tank; each module, in turn, is made up of 106 small batteries, for a total of 5,088 batteries. Engineers were able improve battery technology so that the eBox required fewer batteries than the tzero did.

The Scion xB's entire exhaust system, including the tailpipe, the muffler, and the catalytic converter, simply disappears. So do all the polluting fumes. The eBox produces no gases, and the electric motor is so quiet that most of the time you can hardly hear it at all.

Before the eBox is ready for the road, however, engineers need to make one final change. They replace the gas gauge on the dashboard with a gauge showing how much energy is left in the battery. This way drivers know when they need to recharge their eBox.

# Chapter 3
# eBox Technology

When engineers at AC Propulsion decided to use an existing car for the eBox rather than build a car from the wheels up, they saved themselves a lot of trouble. Much of the difficult technology needed to power the electric car had already been perfected in the tzero.

Engineers then tackled the air conditioning, power windows, power steering, and a state-of-the-art sound system. The electric motor had to supply power to these features without compromising the eBox's driving performance.

Finally, in the summer of 2006, the first eBox **prototype** was ready. By the end of 2006, the eBox was available to the public. In fact, the very first eBox was delivered in February 2007 to electric-car enthusiast and actor Tom Hanks.

◀ **Actor and director Tom Hanks became the proud owner of the first eBox on February 15, 2007.**

## HOW THE EBOX WORKS

Driving an eBox is similar to driving any car. To get moving, the driver simply steps on the accelerator pedal. This activates the controller in the power electronics unit, which regulates the flow of electricity from the batteries to the motor. The harder the driver presses the accelerator, the faster the motor spins and the faster the car goes.

Because the eBox is so quiet, and because the motor can reach maximum power so quickly, drivers have found that it takes a little practice to keep from stepping on the accelerator pedal too hard. It is easy to start speeding without realizing it, and the eBox is capable of a brisk 95 mph (153 km/h).

One interesting difference between the eBox and a conventional car is that the eBox is equipped with a **regenerative braking** system. When the driver takes his or her foot off the accelerator, energy from the moving wheels is changed into electrical energy and transferred back to the battery. The more energy the wheels send back to the battery, the faster the car slows down.

In the eBox, you can adjust the regenerative braking system so that lifting your foot off the accelerator will slow down the car quickly. With some practice, a driver can learn to use the regular brake pedal very rarely.

The eBox also needs less maintenance than a gasoline or hybrid car. There are fewer moving parts to worry about, and there is no need for routine tasks like oil changes. However, it does need some daily attention. Just like a cell phone, a laptop, or an iPod, an eBox needs to have its battery pack charged regularly.

Fortunately, drivers can plug the eBox in almost anywhere. Its recharging cord can attach to any 110-volt household outlet and completely recharge the batteries in about five hours. A 220-volt outlet, such as the type used for an electric dryer, can recharge the battery in about two hours.

Some states have even installed public charging stations where people can plug in their electric or plug-in hybrid vehicles if they are traveling or need to charge the battery before going home.

With a fully charged battery, the eBox can travel 120 miles (193 km) on the highway or 150 miles (241 km) in the city before it needs to be recharged. But if time is a problem, AC Propulsion employees say, a simple thirty-minute charge will enable the eBox to travel 20 to 50 miles (32 to 80 km).

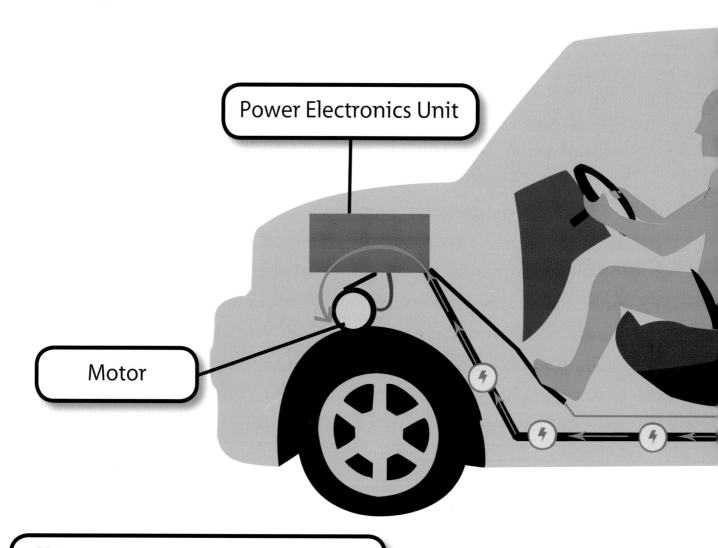

Power Electronics Unit

Motor

**Key**

⚡ Electricity
→ Electricity from the battery
→ Signal from the controller

Battery

When a driver presses the accelerator, a signal is sent to the controller—the computer located in the power electronics unit—to increase the amount of electricity flowing from the battery to the motor. This powers the rotation of the motor, which in turn powers the wheels so the car moves.

## VEHICLE-TO-GRID TECHNOLOGY

In addition to a revamped battery pack, the eBox boasts a feature that may become very important in making battery-powered cars affordable and desirable. The eBox comes equipped with a battery charger that works two ways—not only can it deliver electricity to the battery, it can also take electricity from the battery and deliver it back to the electric company. Engineers call this technology vehicle-to-grid, or V2G.

Why would a car owner want to send electricity back to where it came from? The short answer is because electricity is valuable, and returning what you don't need could save a significant amount of money.

The cost of electricity varies throughout the day. It is least expensive at night, when most offices are closed and most people are asleep. That is also the time, naturally, when an eBox owner is most likely to charge his or her car. During the day, on the other hand, the demand for electricity is high and so is the price.

Sometimes, electric companies need a quick blast of extra power to make sure that people have enough. It is convenient for them, and cheaper, to have a ready supply of electricity rather than to generate more.

Several countries have public charging stations. Drivers can plug in their electric vehicles for a quick charge.

A single plugged-in eBox, may not be able to supply much juice back to the **electric grid**, but many thousands of plugged-in cars could. In effect, an eBox owner could "sell" some unneeded electricity back to the electric company for more than he or she paid for it. By doing this regularly, eBox owners could both reduce the cost of keeping their cars charged and lessen the need for the electric company to produce more electricity.

# Chapter 4
# An Electric Future?

For now, the idea of thousands of eBox owners banding together to sell electricity back to the power companies is a fantasy. There are only dozens of eBoxes on the road, not thousands.

But this is in keeping with AC Propulsion's plans. According to the company, the eBox will remain a conversion, and not become a production car. The eBox is meant to show the public—and the giant car companies—just how good an electric car can be.

If enough people eventually want to drive a battery-powered car, the company reasons, the major automakers will begin mass-producing them, and the cars will become more affordable. In the

◀ **A 2006 eBox parked in front of a windfarm. Some power plants produce electricity from wind power.**

meantime, AC Propulsion is happy to sell its technology to other companies and to continue its research into making even better electric drive systems and batteries.

Many carmakers have, in fact, turned to AC Propulsion for systems to try out in experimental electric cars. Among them are Tesla Motors, which plans to sell its Tesla Model S, an electric sedan, in 2011; Volkswagen, which has experimented with an electric Jetta; and BMW, which is using an AC Propulsion system in its Mini E, an electric version of the Mini Cooper.

Tesla Motors uses a drive system developed by AC Propulsion in its sporty electric roadster.

## GREEN CARS FOR A GREENER COUNTRY

Between the cost of oil and the concern about the environment, hybrids are becoming more popular—and more common—in the United States. All-electric cars, unlike hybrids, use no gasoline at all and therefore do not give off greenhouse gases. This means that they would be even better for Americans' wallets and the environment, right?

Well, maybe. Critics point out that an all-electric car does not mean that the greenhouse gas problem goes away. The electricity the cars depend on must be generated by power plants, and many of those power plants produce tons of greenhouse gases. Exactly how green electric cars are depends on how green the electricity-producing companies are.

Electricity is generated in a number of ways. In some places, electricity comes from burning coal, which releases a lot of carbon dioxide. In other places, electricity comes from nuclear power plants, which produce few greenhouse gases. But they leave us with dangerous radioactive material that somehow must be stored safely for tens of thousands of years.

Other power plants burn oil, which of course is the problem electric cars are meant to solve. Finally, some electricity is produced cleanly by the power of wind turning large windmills or by solar cells using only the light from the Sun.

Figuring out just how much electric cars might help in reducing greenhouse gases is very complicated. Calculations show that because electric cars operate very efficiently, a switch from gasoline power to electric power would lower the amount of greenhouse gases somewhat, no matter how the electricity is produced.

But even if everyone in America drives an electric car, like the eBox, the country will still be producing massive amounts of greenhouse gases. In order to have a substantial effect, a switch to electric cars must go along with a huge effort to build and operate cleaner electric plants.

## SPEED BUMPS

Despite the environmental benefits of electric cars, a couple of problems still block the way of electric cars. One is the distance they can go without recharging. The eBox's range is impressive—120 to 150 miles (193 to 241 km)—and it would more than satisfy most drivers' needs.

In the United States, approximately eight out of every ten people drive 40 miles (64 km) a day or less. For them the eBox would never run out of juice before they got home to recharge it. But what about longer trips? Driving the 225 miles (362 km) from, say, New York City to Washington, D.C., would mean at least one recharging stop each

## Greenest of the Green

Recharging options and battery life are problems for some electric-car owners. However, businessman Shai Agassi and his company, Better Place, based in Palo Alto, California, have proposed a possible solution. Agassi wants to build a chain of charger-equipped garages where car owners could plug their cars in while they're at home or at work.

In addition, the company would build battery-switching stations along highways. At these stations, a robot would take out the used battery and pop in a charged one in just minutes. The batteries would all be owned by the company. Customers would rent them and just pay for the electricity they use. Futhermore, all the electricity supplied by the company would be generated by green methods such as solar panels or wind power.

French carmaker Renault thinks the idea will work and is building electric cars to suit Agassi's robots. So far, Israel and Denmark have already embraced the plan. Australia, Hawaii, and California may follow.

Is it a xB or an eBox? You can't tell from a quick glance. It's what's under the hood that makes all the difference!

way. And few people would be happy to spend hours mid-trip waiting for their car to recharge.

Even at home, recharging is not necessarily as simple as it might sound. In large cities many people live in apartments or in homes without garages. Dangling an extension cord out the window of your fifteenth-floor apartment to charge your car is not really a good option. Neither is removing the battery and hauling it upstairs—the eBox's battery pack weighs 600 pounds (272 kg).

Finally there is the cost. The price of a Scion xB is about $15,000. To convert the car to an eBox takes another $55,000. So anyone wishing to quietly zip along in an eBox must be able to afford to pay $70,000. Of course, once delivered, the eBox saves money on fuel. The electricity needed to take it 150 miles (241 km) costs less than a quarter of the equivalent amount of gasoline. Even so, the eBox will cost its owner far more than a gas-powered car.

None of these problems is impossible to solve. The cost of electric cars will certainly drop if big carmakers start manufacturing them by the tens of thousands. Environmental concerns are forcing power companies to build cleaner electric plants anyway, with or without electric cars. There are also many companies doing research on new kinds of batteries that can hold more energy for longer drives, and on batteries that can recharge in less time.

AC Propulsion employees are devoted to proving that electric cars are reliable and practical.

Whether this will all result in an electric-car America is not certain. But many other countries are betting on the electric car for the future. First among them is China, which has announced that it intends to become the world's largest producer of electric cars by 2012.

At the moment electric cars manufactured by Chinese-based companies are not as good as those made by American or European automakers, but they are improving quickly. And the Chinese companies will likely be able to make the cars for much less money. The technology is certainly improving rapidly, and many foreign and domestic companies, including AC Propulsion, already have factories in China.

Across the planet, people have come to agree that the world of the past century, a world dominated by gasoline-powered cars, is coming to an end. There is less agreement on just what the world of the future will look like, or how quickly it will arrive. But someday soon, somewhere, someone is going to come up with the answer. And it will probably be partly made possible by the innovations made while building the eBox.

# Vital Stats

## EBOX

Battery Type: lithium-ion

Curb Weight: 2,970 lbs (1,347 kg)

Seats: 5

Top Speed: 95 mph (153 km/h)

0–60 mph (0–97 km/h): 7 seconds

Battery Charge Range: 135 miles (127 km)

Recharge Time: 5 hours

# 2009 SCION XB

Power: 158 hp

Curb Weight: 3,086 lbs (1,400 kg)

Seats: 5

Top Speed: 124 mph (200 km/h)

0–60 mph (0–97 km/h): 7.8 seconds

Average Fuel Economy: 25 mpg (10.6 km/l)

# Glossary

**alternative fuels**  Substances, other than gasoline and other petroleum products, that can be used to power engines.

**atmosphere**  The air surrounding Earth.

**climate**  The average weather of a place over many years.

**compressed**  Squeezed together; in the case of the life-forms that became oil, they were pressed together over millions of years by layers of rock and soil.

**converts**  To make alterations to a vehicle in order to change it from a gasoline-powered car to an electric car.

**decomposed**  Broken down into parts or basic elements; when plants or animals die, because of time, weather, and the action of insects and bacteria, they are broken down.

**drive system**  The parts of a car, including its engine or motor, that make it move.

**efficient**  Functioning without much waste or unnecessary effort.

**electric grid**  The network of power lines from which all electricity users draw power.

**environment**  The rock, soil, air, and water that sustains all life, as well as the life-forms they sustain.

| | |
|---|---|
| **fuel cell** | A device that changes a chemical fuel, such as hydrogen, into electrical energy, which can power a vehicle. |
| **global warming** | An increase in Earth's average yearly temperature that is believed to be caused by pollution and that results in climate changes. |
| **greenhouse gas** | A gas, such as carbon dioxide, that contributes to global warming. |
| **organisms** | Living things. |
| **power train** | The part in a car that transmits power from the engine to the wheels. |
| **prototype** | The original or model on which something is based or formed. |
| **range** | The distance a vehicle can travel before needing to refuel or recharge. |
| **regenerative braking** | A system that allows the heat produced off when a car brakes to be changed into electricity, which can be stored in the battery. |

# Further Information

**BOOKS**

Bearce, Stephanie. *Tell Your Parents All about Electric and Hybrid Cars.* Hockessin, DE: Mitchell Lane Publishers, 2009.

Cherry, Lynne and Gary Braasch. *How We Know What We Know About Our Changing Climate: Scientists and Kids Explore Global Warming.* Nevada City, CA: Dawn Publications, 2008.

Solway, Andrew. *Generating and Using Electricity.* Why Science Matters. Chicago, IL: Heinemann Library, 2009.

Welsbacher, Anne. *Earth-Friendly Design.* Saving Our Living Earth. New York: Lerner, 2008.

## WEBSITES

**AC Propulsion**'s website provides information about the technology the company's engineers have developed and the vehicles in which it is used.

www.acpropulsion.com

**Energy Kids**, a website run by the Energy Information Administration, provides information about energy use in the United States.

http://tonto.eia.doe.gov/kids/

**Energy Quest** is the California Energy Commission's guide to alternative fuel vehicles. There is information on cars that run on gasoline, hydrogen, electricity, and biodiesel, as well as links to sources with more information.

www.energyquest.ca.gov/transportation/

**Science News for Kids**'s article "Ready, Unplug, Drive" has lots of information about plug-in and electric cars.

www.sciencenewsforkids.org/articles/20081029/Feature1.asp

# Index

The page numbers in **boldface** are photographs, illustrations, or diagrams.

# Index

# About the Author

Marc Zabludoff, former editor in chief of *Discover* magazine, has been involved in communicating science to the public for more than two decades. He is the author of all ten titles in Marshall Cavendish's recent series Prehistoric Beasts. His other work for Marshall Cavendish includes *Spiders*, *Beetles*, *Monkeys* in the AnimalWays series, as well as *The Insect Class*, *The Reptile Class*, and *The Protoctist Kingdom* in the series Family Trees.